Intimate Bureaucracies

INTIMATE BUREAUCRACIES

A Manifesto

dj readies

punctum books ✶ brooklyn, ny

INTIMATE BUREAUCRACIES: A MANIFESTO
© Craig J. Saper (dj readies), 2012.

This work is licensed under the Creative Commons Attribution-NonCommerical-NoDerivs 3.0 Unported License. To view a copy of this license, visit: http://creativecommons.org/licenses/by-nc-nd/3.0, or send a letter to Creative Commons, 444 Castro Street, Suite 900, Mountain View, California, 94041, USA.

First published in 2012 by
punctum books
Brooklyn, New York

In collaboration with:

AK Press Tactical Media, Baltimore / Oakland / Edinburgh
The AK Press Tactical Media Project makes short, timely political interventions freely available in download and zine form (http://www.revolutionbythebook.akpress.org/ak-tactical-media/).

Minor Compositions, Wivenhoe / Brooklyn / Port Watson
Minor Compositions is a series of interventions & provocations drawing from autonomous politics, avant-garde aesthetics, and the revolutions of everyday life (http://www.minorcompositions.info/).

punctum books is dedicated to radically creative modes of intellectual inquiry and writing across a whimsical para-humanities assemblage. This is a space for the imp-orphans of thought and pen, an ale-serving church for little vagabonds (http://punctumbooks.com).

ISBN-13: 978-0615612034

Facing-page drawing by Heather Masciandaro.

Intimate Bureaucracies: A Manifesto

dj readies

Participatory decentralization, a mantra of art and political networks, expresses a peculiarly intimate bureaucratic form. These forms of organization represent a paradoxical mix of artisanal production, mass-distribution techniques, and a belief in the democratizing potential of electronic and mechanical reproduction techniques. Borrowing from mass-culture image banks, these intimate bureaucracies play on forms of publicity common in societies of spectacles and public relations. Intimate bureaucracies have no demands, no singular ideology, nor righteous path.

Intimate bureaucracies monitor the pulse of the society of the spectacle and the corporatized bureaucracies: economics, as in Big Business; culture, as in Museums and Art Markets; mass media, as in

INTIMATE BUREAUCRACIES

Studio Systems and Telecommunication Networks; and politics, as in Big Government. Rather than simply mounting a campaign against big conglomerations of business, government, and culture, these intimate bureaucracies and their works use the forms of corporate bureaucracies for intimate ends. Rather than reach the lowest common denominator, they seek to construct what those in the business world would call niche marketing to specific, narrowly defined demographics. Ironically, the model these artists developed has now become the new mantra of businesses interested in utilizing the World Wide Web and the Internet, as these technologies allow for very specific niche marketing. Intimate bureaucracies emulate, and resist, the very systems of the new business model used in Internet marketing. George Maciunas's FluxHouse project functioned like a DIY development corporation, but with cooperative and social capitalists motivations. Maciunas referred to it as entrepreneurial communism, but now the phrase social entrepreneurs describes similar projects like the Kiva or Kickstarter projects.

The apparent oxymoron, intimate bureaucracies, is a set of strategically subversive maneuvers and also the very basis for the new productive mythology surrounding the World Wide Web. Electronic networks combine a bureaucracy with its codes, passwords, links, and so on with niche marketing, intimate personal contacts, and the like, creating a hybrid situation or performance. It's a mix of cold impersonal systems and intimate social connections; it scales up whispering down the lane games. The earlier projects of Anna Freud Banana, Guy Bleus (whose canceling stamps appear in this manifesto), Randall Packer, Geof Huth, and many others all used the trappings of bureaucracies, like canceling stamps,

dj readies

systems of organizing information, and alternative publication networks, to create similar hybrid performances. The Madison, Wisconsin artists mIEKAL aND & Lyx Ish even started a Dreamtime Village (www.dreamtimevillage.org). It is not merely business or governmental performance masquerading as performance art. It is not even performance art mocking business and government procedures, but the emergence of an alternative politics.

Early in his career, Roland Barthes used the image of a car trip through history to describe how mythology works. When a driver looks out of a car's windshield, she sees the landscape as full and present, and, at the same time, she sees the windshield. Myths function as windows framing and mediating our view of the world around us. The slightest change in focus allows the driver to notice the window. A broken window makes the myth too obvious, and we seek new myths. To focus only on the window would cause the car to crash. Barthes suggests a third option besides naïveté or cynical nihilism. Focusing on window and view separately goes against myth's dynamic of both window and scenery taken in together. Barthes explains that when he counters this dynamic, he morphs from a reader to that of mythologist. The mythologist takes advantage of the vacillation between noticing the windowpane and seeing the landscape to create what he calls an artificial mythology. This counter-myth of "naïveté looked at" neither replaces the window nor transcends it to direct access (*Mythologies*, 136). It simply changes the driver's focus.

Barthes does not tell us much more about this phrase, nor does he allude to it ever again in his other works throughout his career. From this little detail, this little thrown-away gem—or as the Spanish refer to a diamond in a lemon, a *sapates*—springs the possibility of a methodology for the study of cultural and media invention.

That Barthes chose a drive in a car as the model for ideology seems particularly fitting for citizens of the United States because the American Dream depends so much on the mobility of the family car, the destruction of downtown city neighborhoods, and the disruption of walkable communities. Even e-mail and the Internet have failed to dent the car's hold. Bicycles, important means of transportation in many economies remain a recreational vehicle or, in congested urban areas, a way for speedy messengers to get around the car traffic. These daring bike-messengers are the exception that proves the rule: all of our cultural myths seem to circulate around the car, and quite literally. The car is not just as an apt metaphor for mythologies; it is the epitome of American mythologies. The familiarity of the car makes it not only Barthes's vehicle for the metaphor to describe the interactions of myth, artificial myth, and material history, but also an image used in popular culture to describe progress through history.

Intimate bureaucracies may exist on a different scale than the large systems that determine ideologies. One view of the conflict involving the Occupy Wall Street movement (OWS) might suggest a conflict against the large-ideological fossil fuel-burning car (and the socio-political industry) as well as the rapid transport system's corollaries in the instant flows of capital among investment banks. The endless rapid cartel system (pun intended) involves a series of objectionable results, including the flows of capital away from slowly declining red-lined areas.

In response to the OWS protests, the society of the instant produces 24/7 news flashes, rapid summaries and counter-arguments, all clamoring for an instantly available definitive set of "demands" or a

dj readies

"program." The system does not merely demand the attention of the viewers as in the society of the spectacle, but now also demands instant response. OWS's most profound politics may have less to do with the injustices of the current tax codes, wealth disparity, or even, economic collapse, and more to do with its systems and practices of organization and communication.

My book *Networked Art* uses the neologism 'sociopoetic' to describe how artists performed, manipulated, and scored (as in musical scores) social situations. These social situations function as part of an artwork. The networking over, and on, boundaries (national, geographic, political, technological, organizational, cultural, and aesthetic) became, in these works, a canvas. In Randall Packer's "United States Department of Art & Technology," his invented department, complete with signage, photographs of a governmental building with the department's name engraved in stone over the doors, logos, memos, and other trappings of the USDA&T (www.usdat.us), opens on to many other questions. Who owns the right to use the term United States? Should the United States have a cabinet-level department that examines the key component (technology) of our future? How would such a department function? Who determines what departments we need? Why not have a USDA&T? What other departments do we need? Perhaps a US Department of Intimate Bureaucracies (USDIB)?

The term sociopoetic describes the use of social situations or social networks as a canvas. The term sociopoetic does not define my methodology. Instead, the term describes the works studied here. My theoretical approach studies how situations function poetically (or sociopoetically). Although I do present contextual information (the history, the participants,

INTIMATE BUREAUCRACIES

the politics, and the like) as entangled in the artwork, my focus remains on how these works manipulate and score situations. In many of the artworks I have studied previously, the artists created "intimate bureaucracies" that "sought to project intimacy onto otherwise impersonal systems" (*Networked Art*, 24). One might argue that this project seeks to do the same for social action theory. By highlighting the existing aesthetic relationships as well as performance settings, distribution systems, measurement machinery, or the social apparatus, my project does not demythologize, but displaces, the frame to focus on the sociopoetic dimension. Scholars usually describe that dimension as a mechanism of social control and manipulation. Whether one agrees or disagrees with the justification or results of that social apparatus, it is commonly considered only in social scientific terms rather than as a poetic and artistic practice or a social poetry. Bureaucracy, as a mode of governmental or corporate organization, depends on officials rather than elected representatives or charismatic leaders. It usually connotes a cold, faceless, and excessively complicated system of administration. It epitomizes the distance between a governing body's procedures and the needs and desires of its citizens, subjects, or customers. Of course, much of the term's descriptive power depends on its connotations rather than on its specific meaning and definitions. It also suggests a large-scale mechanism familiar to anyone who has lived through modernity in the twentieth century. In tragic situations, it has Kafkaesque overtones and the markings of fascism—what Hannah Arendt called the "banality of evil." In happier situations, it appears in the administration of postal systems, the protocols of the Internet, and even IKEA's distribution systems. It never finds itself describing radical forms of social organization.

dj readies

Intimacy, the close familiarity of friendship or love, by definition depends on a small-scale system of communication. Its warmth, face-to-face contact, and fleeting impact has often been the subject of art and literature. It usually appears in administration situations as either an insincere ornamentation of a political campaign ("pressing the flesh" or kissing babies) or as inappropriate office behavior (affairs, gossip, etc.), but rarely as the center of a political system. The "small is beautiful" movement did suggest the possibility of an intimacy in politics, but did not provide a blueprint for how to scale the system to the size of a government.

The pseudonymously written *bolo'bolo* (1983), published by Semiotext(e) in their conspiratorial-sounding Foreign Agents series, describes the practical steps toward a utopian international social system. The author known only as "p.m." (at least before post-publication interviews revealed the author's identity) explains how small groups gathering outside the functions of an economy will form the foundation of this new social system. Instead of impersonal production and consumption, in which people's work, for an abstract economy, defines the social system, people join together only in groups of common enthusiasms. No group, or "bolo," forces anyone to stay, and individuals move from group to group depending on their current enthusiasm. The examples of common enthusiasms listed by p.m. include a very wide, and endlessly elastic, range of interests: garli-bolo, blue-bolo, coca-bolo, no-bolo, retro-bolo, les-bolo, etc.

The bolo depends on limiting social organizations to groups of between five hundred and one thousand persons so that they do not become dependent on higher authorities. In traditional governments or other organizations, a separate larger administrative group is

Intimate Bureaucracies

a "structurally necessitated bureaucracy." In that governing system, any administrative and governing body probably works to assure the citizens that they can meet the specific group's needs. Functioning governments seeks to serve the needs of its citizens. The bolos seek to avoid these well-meaning "control organs" that become "susceptible to corruption," and require constant vigilance and work for an abstract labor market. p.m. also argues that bolos do not use "the large communes of the 1970s" as models. Instead, bolos function as "civil member organizations" in which you can "bring your wealth in with you" and "take it out with you when you leave. They are not communes" (*bolo'bolo*, 85).

For the purposes of this manifesto, the current role of technology in society suggests that intimate networks may have unwittingly initiated a reconfiguration of sociopolitical systems that looks much like a bolo. Although p.m. insists that bolo'bolo will "not be an electronic civilization" because "computers are typical for centralized, depersonalized systems," s/he goes on to explain that "the existing material and hardware could also be used by the bolos for certain purposes" because "networks are energy- efficient and permit a better horizontal contact between users than other media" (*bolo'bolo*, 124). Written before the implications of online communication were at all apparent, p.m. thinks of a network "connected with regional or planetary processors or data-banks" (*bolo'bolo*, 123). Once the transportation system slows and centralized

dj readies

systems of control fail, electronic networks will allow for communication to continue. In a description that could easily apply to social media, p.m. explains the impact of this type of network:

> Such a network of horizontal communication could be an ideal complement to self-sufficiency. Independence doesn't have to become synonymous with isolation. For the bolos there's little risk of becoming dependent upon technology and specialists—they can always fall back on their own expertise and personal contacts. (Without bolos and relative autarky, computer technology is just a means of control by the centralized machine.) (*bolo'bolo*, 125)

These radical systems already exist in OWS and in online communities and interest groups; and, just as p.m. suspected, they would begin without regard to economics, but rather in terms of shared enthusiasms. The impact, though, transcends an art project or a collective activity. It has become the foundation of much more broad platforms for cultural invention and social action.

Intimate bureaucracies, and other distributed weaves of networks online, unwittingly move toward appreciating even the most powerful government's lack of power as a threat, rather than as a revolutionary's ultimate dream-come-true. Lack of power (or power to attack only), rather than the ability to defend, preserve, and protect, may define contemporary culture's greatest threat. If, as the Fascists say, the trains always ran on time in Mussolini's Italy, then, one might answer, they ran only for the Fascists. In the contemporary version of that tautology, the escape plans and contingencies worked in the flooding of New Orleans by Hurricane Katrina, for example, but only for those that escaped. Intimate networks respond by setting up online networks, and even the most frivolous enthusiasms, like knitting or craft sites, prepare the participants.

Media studies, as a discipline, seeks to demonstrate how media forms and messages position, manipulate, and delude subjects. The networked sociopoetic experiments do not celebrate this absence as some kind of resistance; rather, they suggest an alternative to exposés, de-mythologies, and revelations. Those alternatives do not replace readings that find effaced politics lurking behind simple presentations, but focus instead on incompetence masquerading as power and authority, rather than on ideological power masquerading as entertainment, culture, and media. Intimate networks offer connectedness and shared responsibility in the face of a lack of power. They often explicitly discuss their collective efforts as "underground" alternatives to corporate power.

The aesthetics of connectedness, the focus on concrete enthusiasms, the links and movement among the enthusiasts' groups, and the willing manipulation of desires (not for productive economic ends) make the networked art experiments into a model for, and demonstration of, cultural invention and social action. The aesthetics, or sociopoetics, of tribe-making activities has subtle and very specific qualities. Looking only at the quantitative, or explicit, will miss appreciating the torque, frisson, and mood of those links. Although the databases of these hyper-linked tribal forms are limited and relatively small, and the actual links usually number less than one thousand at any given time, the cognitive map—the imagined—unfolds as aninfinity of possibilities. Preparing the mind for that type of imagination is an ongoing

dj readies

project.
Fluxus (www.fluxus.org), now included as a canonical movement in art history, was intended first as the name of a publication, and later as a social experiment. The most famous of those who participated in Fluxus projects, events, and publications were John Lennon and Yoko Ono, but the core members, like Joseph Beuys (1921-1986) and the group's founder, George Maciunas (1931-1978), possessed an interest in social systems that was extremely influential in contemporary arts. Outside of museums, galleries, art history, and among contemporary experimental artists and poets, Fluxus is little known to scholars of political, cultural, and social action. Certainly, compared to the term Happenings or the seemingly more politically engaged Yippies, Fluxus and Maciunas have remained a footnote as a social program.

Fluxus's goal was to purge the art world of authors and creative geniuses. Like many of the contributions to assembling magazines, the works became models for alternative forms of social organization. Indeed, as Estera Milman explains, "Fluxus work (objects, paperworks, publications, festivals, and performances) and the movement's social structures became congruent and interchangeable" (Milman 12). George Maciunas's manifesto for Fluxus explains this socio-poetic practice:

> Fluxus [...] forgoes distinction between art and non-art forgoes artist's indispensability, exclusiveness, individuality, ambition, . . . (Maciunas, "Manifesto," n.p.)

The Fluxus project combined a sometimes parodic emulation of the Bauhaus model, with the production of "impersonal" conceptual games and puzzles, concrete poetry, along with an interest in situations, experimental culture, and an attack on "commodity value" in art. These concerns and the mixing of these tendencies appeared in a number of Fluxus assemblings and periodicals. While Vaudeville, Cage, and Duchamp have secured prominent places in scholarship on art and mass culture, Spike Jones still remains a somewhat marginal figure. Yet, his "Musical Depreciation Revue" offers a whole array of useful jokes, gags, puns, spoonerisms, and the like.

The overlap of Fluxus art and social programs began in their event scores. Fluxus event scores and performance instructions have a didactic structural grammar; they seem to be parodies of social-scientific experiments simply because they reduce theatricality to a set of instructions. Using the trappings of a social experiment suggests a way to further displace the interpretation of Fluxus as an art movement. Building and interacting with their work, rather than passively appreciating it as a finished product, changes interpretation into a generative project. The start of that sort of interpretation begins with a new concept: intimate bureaucracy.

One sees an important allusion to intimate bureaucracies in Dick Higgins's mail-art collaboration in 1989 with Robert Rehfeldt, an East German artist. Higgins, a composer who studied with Henry Cowell and John Cage, produced a series of Fluxus scores and events starting in the early 1960s. He became an

dj readies

influential publisher, poet, art historian of visual poetry, essayist and theorist, and an artist. The swath of connections from the one collaboration with Rehfeldt includes the authenticating rubber-stamp of a Polish Communist Party official in charge of approving, censoring, or rejecting art events as well as Higgins's identical stamp. Higgins's notes and correspondence with Rehfeldt would illuminate one Party official's continuing rejection of mail-art events and exhibitions in Poland; the map would also include plans for duplicating and distributing the authenticating stamp to Polish mail-artists, who, in turn, approved exhibitions.

The stamps also connect to the odd obsessive paranoia about mail-art in the Eastern Block nations, as evidenced by East Germany's Stasi, who had an enormous mail-art collection from their investigations and confiscations. The mapping of the mail-art event included Higgins's descriptions of how he also subscribed to gay porn magazines and Trotskyist newspapers, both prohibited by the Communist Party, using the name and address of the Party censor, whose authenticating stamp they had duplicated. The narrative of the map would also include the uncharacteristically formal and typed letter from Rehfeldt to Higgins saying that "Mr. Higgins had performed an inappropriate act" by using the fraudulent stamp to apparently approve a whole series of mail-art events and exhibitions in Poland. Next to the formal letter, another unsigned, handwritten note sent to Higgins from East Germany simply says, "Keep it up!" The mail-art event also connects to the issues of the Commonpress assembling (so named because of the common effort of the contributors) that were produced in Poland and assembled by Pawel Petasz, who explained that the Polish censors would stamp the back of each and every proof page of a publication with an official mark of approval or rejection. Rubber stamp art from around the world was the focus of all the issues produced in Poland.

The branching nodes of the Rehfeldt-Higgins map would also include Higgins's writings on the post-cognitive mode of research that appears in his books and essays on intermedia as well as his writings on mail-art. Other branches of the map would include Ben Vautier's "Postman's Choice" and other Fluxus mail-art. Conceptually, the Higgins-Rehfeldt mail-art event would also link to descriptions and examples of unwanted direct-mail and spam email, even though the term did not appear until the 1990s. One could imagine links to theories of paranoia, and various artistic uses in, for example, the Surrealists' "paranoiac criticism." Other nodes would include Ray Johnson's use of paranoid systems in his mail-art and on-sendings (discussed below) as well as the secondary literature on hysterical and paranoid modernism. This example of a swath of networked nodes illustrates the value of the mapping of ideas, objects, events, people, systems, and locations in terms of an intimate bureaucracy. Just exhibiting the stamp would not do justice to the vast sprawl of this sociopoetic project.

The Occupy Wall Street (OWS) movement starting in the second decade of the twenty-first century is a model of social organization, an intimate bureaucracy, that coalesces beyond any particular protest or set of

dj readies

demands. The demand for goals, for political and policy objectives, distracts and elides the value of OWS whether one agrees with the protests or not. The demonstration of a working model of an intimate bureaucracy threatens the dominant model of social organization. The privately owned "public park" where the OWS occupied the space for their protest's home base in New York City (Zuccotti Park) required a city permit for microphones and other forms of amplification. When a speaker decides to address the crowd, the crowd repeats the phrase, "MIC check," to call everyone to attention, especially those out of earshot of the speaker. Constraints encourage invention: hence those that can hear the speaker repeat the words so those farther back in the crowd can hear; and those farther back from the speaker repeat, in turn, the phrases just as they hear them. There is sometimes an echo and a time lag as the horizontal amplification reaches those farther away in waves. Usually, the collective chant-repetition of the speaker's phrases simply amplifies the words so that the entire crowd of hundreds can hear. The practice resembles call and response in churches as well as the rote repetition in the scholastic tradition of the Middle Ages. This style of protest, horizontal amplification, extends the normal logos, ethos, and pathos of cultural broadcast and rhetoric by examining a choral response that is absent from descriptions of communication except as a moral warning against "mob psychology."

In the occupation of 'public' space by pedestrians, none of the commentaries have noted that public protest involves protest marches on foot, not in cars; it is just too obvious to note—too much on the surface of the events unfolding. Taking up a "pedestrian" cause (in one sense, an exemplification of the criticism of OWS as failing to inspire the public with clear goals, solutions, and mainstream politics), with their slow media microphone check, inherently opposes the grand narrative theory, the car-vehicle-of-ideology, a rejection of financial cartels, not with a bigger and better Political Utility Vehicle, but with an intimate bureaucracy and horizontal amplification. Politics, protest, and even the grand narratives of sexuality find themselves challenged by the byke-sexual and masswalkist.

The 1960s witnessed the success of one significant intimate bureaucracy when George Maciunas (born Jurgis Maciunas in Lithuania) encouraged and helped initiate the artists' co-op movement and the street festivals that eventually led to the vitalization of the up-until-then distressed and crumbling New York City neighborhood now known as SoHo (and at the time also included part of Little Italy). Although Maciunas had studied architecture at Cooper Union and Carnegie Institute, he is widely known as the founder of the Fluxus productions and events. Fluxus, in the context of public space, urban design, and the social organization of everyday life, changes its disciplinary category from art history to history-arts (arts as in *ars* or practice). Maciunas issued a "proposed propaganda action" in the April 6, 1963 "Fluxus News-Policy Letter, No. 6" when he listed the following goals of the group: "a) Pickets and demonstrations; b) Sabotage and disruption; c) Compositions; d) Sale of Fluxus publications." This score for future events changes the placing of Fluxus from considering it only as a historical art movement to appreciating it as a strategy for social action and organization as a sociopoetics.

dj readies

The artist-owned cooperatives in industrial buildings in downtown New York City had begun in the early 1960s. The start of this movement was a series of lucky coincidences. In 1963, Jane Jacobs noticed a sign on a building at Greenwich and 12th Street. The sign explained that the building was about to be seized for tax arrears and the sign was announcing the eventual auction of the property. She quickly formed the Citizens for Artists Housing (CAH), and her group eventually bought the building. Mayor Wagner agreed to limit the price of the building to forty-five thousand dollars as part of his Renaissance Act, and Jack Kaplan, whose daughter had recently married a downtown artist, funded the initial purchase. Soon after CAH made the purchase, an Artists Tenants Association (ATA) was formed to handle the applications for admittance into the building. Charles Simpson explains that a city code, Article 7-B, was "utilized only for this one building before subsequent amendments broadened its scope, established the principle that loft living could be made legal and responsible, and that working artists held a separate priority for this type of residence" (*Soho*, 155). Three years later, Maciunas entered the artists' cooperative scene, and made it a larger and more deliberate program with a Fluxus-inflected sociopoetic goal of emancipation.

In 1966, George Maciunas founded Fluxhouse Cooperatives, Inc. and established himself as president. His Fluxhouse designs went beyond co-op lofts and studios to include collective workshops, food buying, and theaters. His goals, explicitly connected to intermedia, a term Dick Higgins used to describe works that fell conceptually between media and disciplines, sought to "link the strength of various media together" and to connect artist communities with larger public and social culture. He too approached Jack Kaplan and the JM Kaplan Fund. Maciunas asked for two thousand dollars: half from the Fund and half from Kaplan himself (Simpson, *Soho*, 156). The first Fluxhouse purchase was 80-82 Wooster Street, and by August of 1967 it was fully subscribed. Maciunas's corporation made a cash down-payment, and the former owner assumed the mortgage. Each artist contributed two thousand dollars up front and paid a $205-per-month maintenance fee. The lofts were 3,300 square feet. By June of 1968, Maciunas and his Fluxhouse Cooperatives, Inc. had sponsored co-ops on Prince, Broome, and along West Broadway, occupying seventeen buildings with eleven cooperatives. Before the artists' cooperative movement and Fluxhouse began, many feared the area would slide further into an industrial slum, and after the expressway project was canceled and as the cooperatives changed the area to a more desirable mixed-use neighborhood, prices climbed fifty percent very quickly. Eventually, the corporate entity that Maciunas used to buy and convert the buildings to co-ops needed a name to distinguish it from any single building; Maciunas called it Good Deal Realty Corp.

Maciunas wanted the neighborhood to serve as a haven for artistic and collective experiments in living. Others did not want its zoning, control, or meaning to change. The zoning laws, initially part of progressive efforts to force employers to not house workers in sweatshops, made working and living in many SoHo buildings illegal. Those zoning ordinances later protected small factories and businesses from the escalating rents in residential neighborhoods. By the

dj readies

1960s, factories had moved out, and the property values were relatively inexpensive, especially after the planned construction of the Lower Manhattan Expressway had lowered property values. Maciunas and the co-operatively organized artists were able to buy these buildings, but because George, if not all of the other artists involved, saw these projects as part of their own artistic re-invention of the neighborhood, they were reluctant to hire mob-controlled contractors or give kickbacks and bribes common in the building trades. Also, Maciunas produced "endless and minutely detailed projections of renovation costs," and soon his vision and Fluxhouse ideals began to clash with other realities, including city rules and the needs of the actual artists involved in the cooperatives.

In his first-hand reminiscence about the emergence of SoHo as an artist colony in the 1960s, Richard Kostelanetz describes Maciunas and the Fluxhouse Cooperatives Project. He describes in detail who lived where, and what rents were then (and now). Maciunas, in Kostelanetz's account, was not someone even artists would necessarily invite over; yet, they all thrilled at his audacious activities on their behalf, and everyone was talking about one or another of Maciunas's stunts to avoid corporate control or government injunctions (*Soho: Rise and Fall*, 46). He illegally tapped into the electric service, and then hid the wires in a tree on the street. When the city came to cut down the tree, he told them he would photograph them and cutting down a beautiful old tree would make the newspapers; they left, leaving his theft of electricity undiscovered (49). He once chased a city building inspector with a Samurai sword; he avoided capture by the Sheriff's officers by not leaving his apartment until after 5:00 pm, when they would stop serving warrants for the day; and he alluded capture by the police by constructing booby-trapped doors and escape passages. In spite of these escapades, he was building an internationally prominent art group and running his realty business.

Many of the artists did pay bribes not just to the mob, but to city inspectors, and to independent contractors who would sign off on work actually done by the artists themselves. Maciunas wanted to make the renovations a do-it-yourself project much as he wanted to make art projects as do-it-yourself kits. Although part of his motivation was personal and particular to his unwillingness to pay for any service he did not receive, part of his way of thinking about the overall project was influenced by his thinking about Fluxus. Organized crime syndicates opposed his unwillingness to pay kickbacks (and therefore pay homage to their control of the territory) with violent attacks, but miraculously his dreams prevailed. Unfortunately, the injuries Maciunas suffered from one attack led to the loss of one eye, and apparently hastened his death a few years later, and thus Maciunas became a martyr over the use and meaning of a downtown New York City neighborhood. Although the Mob cares not at all about particular uses or meanings of buildings, their insistence on making everyone pay meant that someone's refusal to pay would change the meaning of their power to control the area. Maciunas wanted the area to stand for self-reliant artists, not Mob-indebted or State-controlled renters. Yet, it is clear Maciunas and Fluxus

dj readies

artists considered their work in terms of socially active networks of participants, or as Dick Higgins says, it was "a way of life and death." (Higgins, qtd. Friedman, "Introduction," viii). Downtown New York City was one of their canvases. Maciunas did not intend to direct the final outcome of the neighborhood. He saw his participation in the general move to change the area as an open constraint, a phrase used to describe instruction-like scores for events that performers and readers could follow in their own style and circumstances. On the other hand, he also saw the Fluxhouse project as part of his larger efforts as an artist, and soon his vision would clash with the residents' desires. Problems began at the 16-18 Greene Street cooperative. Kaplan and the National Foundation for the Arts were losing interest in Fluxhouse as they began their own artist housing projects, and the Federal government did not want to back the mortgages because of fire hazards. Given this turn of events, the Fluxhouse residents became increasingly aware that they lacked the philanthropic backing as leverage to obtain the required zoning variances or the occupancy permits from the Department of Buildings. In short, the residents realized they were living in the buildings illegally, and they looked to Fluxhouse Cooperatives, Inc. for answers.

First, the cooperative food buying aspect of Fluxhouse failed in large part because Maciunas had purchased very large quantities of items *he* liked to eat, like Russian black bread, while others involved did not consider those items as essential staples. Second, because he had drawn up low estimates for repairs and renovations, believing in the do-it-yourself ethos, he had undercapitalized the buildings. Third, he had moved money around in unconventional ways that led to charges of corruption. For example, he loaned twenty-six thousand dollars from members' deposits to four other co-ops he was also starting without the depositors' knowledge.

In terms of my argument here, that Fluxhouse was an intermedia and an intimate bureaucracy, Maciunas's justification for the odd to completely illegal accounting practices suggests these larger goals. In the Fluxhouse Newsletter of June 22, 1968, he defended his lending and accounting practices:

> The reason for such disposition of monies is my principle of collectivism—running the cooperatives not necessarily in a legalistically correct way, but in a way to benefit the collective good. When a particular cooperative is in danger of losing a building to foreclosure of lien, every effort—all the funds, go to the rescue. This has worked well without detriment to anybody. Not one of the 4 closings we had so far was delayed by this principle of a "collective chest." It would not have delayed the closing of 465 West Broadway either had it not been for the interference of the "shadow kitchen." (qtd. Simpson, *Soho*, 159)

Of course, in historical terms commentators have frowned on Maciunas's cavalier attitude, and the cooperative's members began at the time to become autonomous, severing ties to Maciunas. The key phrase in this defense of the unconventional accounting practices, "not necessarily in a legalistically correct way, but in a way to benefit the collective good," might also serve to describe the larger Fluxus ethos and sociopoetic goals. The artists associated with Fluxus created works, actions, and

dj readies

events that often involved ways to think though sociopolitical failures as well as suggest alternative living situations as solutions. Against Maciunas's artlike experiment, the shareholders formed what he called a "shadow kitchen" in order to take control of their own buildings. They considered him a swindler guilty of corruption and cronyism, and absurdly stubborn (e.g., co-opers were paying the necessary bribes to fix plumbing problems behind his back). Ken Friedman notes that "it is a disservice to George Maciunas to present him [as] the image of a petty (if lovable) tyrant, a cross between an artistic Stalin and a laughable Breton. . . . [he] was a fabulous organizational technologist" who saw power sharing as an artistic strategy ("Fluxus and Company," 252).

The Fluxhouse situation also suggests a way of working for Maciunas. He took an economic situation and used it as a canvas. For example, Hannah Higgins describes how when Maciunas "was very poor he bought cans of food from the grocery store that had lost their labels. They were, understandably, sold at a considerable discount. Dinner might be string beans, chicken soup or corned-beef hash. The adventure lay in opening the cans to see what was inside. Ben Vautier had these cans relabeled as 'Flux Mystery Food'" ("Fluxus Fortuna," 57).

By late 1968, the Fluxhouse phase of the artists cooperative movement had ended and was replaced by the SoHo Artists Association (SAA) that sought to make the co-ops legal and to give the neighborhood its own name and identity. Soon the artists looked to city planners rather than Maciunas because bureaucratic skills were indispensable. In early May 1970, during Vietnam Moratorium Weekend, and in the wake of the recent killings at Kent State and Jackson State colleges as well as the invasion of Cambodia, the SoHo Artists Festival attracted 70,000 to 100,000 people. The press coverage was enthusiastically positive, noting that the festival, including mock funeral dances, was an affirmation of life during a weekend of national anger and mourning. About six months later, on January 21, 1971, the city of New York officially legalized housing for studio-residences in the forty-three blocks of SoHo.

SoHo, for Maciunas, could serve varied needs, including living, commerce, and entertainment. In the language of urban planners, Fluxus artists and others wanted to create a mixed-use neighborhood from the crumbling post-industrial lofts. Their efforts had to do with a shift in ownership and meaning rather than with constructing new buildings or opposing current systems of legitimate economic exchange. When the now destroyed World Trade Center was first planned and proposed in the mid-1960s, it stood in opposition to the mixed uses that downtown could serve. It would serve high finance commerce only. Ironically, the success of the finance industry drew people to two previously industrial, commerce-only neighborhoods, TriBeCa and Battery Park City, thus making an even lower downtown area a place to live and not just work. In the aftermath of the attack on, and destruction of, the World Trade Center, many planners saw any rebuilding as an opportunity to more successfully connect the old downtown to Battery Park City. That is, just as Maciunas found an opportunity in a decaying downtown neighborhood, we can learn from Fluxus how to convert destruction into an opening for re-envisioning urban space. In that sense,

dj readies

this manifesto can serve as a blueprint, or Fluxprint, to re-build downtown New York City.

One might assume, again incorrectly, that Fluxus artists' interest in collective works and gift exchange festivals like Yam Festivals (1963; the name was borrowed from Potlatch festivals) opposed commerce, capitalism, and real estate deals. As Hannah Higgins notes, an "old-fashioned leftist rhetoric" is "all too often attached to Fluxus as a whole" ("Fluxus Fortuna," 45). Fluxus was never so simple to categorize. When we look at their activities and announcements, their efforts at social networking often involved borrowing business strategies. They did challenge the established gallery system that tended to favor painting, for example, but they packaged their alternative in a storefront model that embraced mercantilism. Their store would sell relatively inexpensive items. Artists, poets, and musicians associated with Fluxus invented businesses—both imaginary (like Nam June Paik's Avant-Garde University of Hinduism) and real, such as Dick Higgins's Something Else Press, Daniel Spoerri's Eat Art Restaurant, George Maciunas's mail-order Fluxshop, and many more.

They did not oppose the financial gain of individuals, but sought to embed those gains in collective efforts and gains. For one contemporary example, Ben Vautier continues to aggressively market his work in the most commercial ways, including putting his signature on bottles of wine. Although some critics have stressed the challenge to capitalism rather than the entrepreneurial aspect, many types of economic models of distribution work simultaneously in Fluxus sociopoetic works.

Fluxus artists, and Fluxhouse specifically, may have failed in the goal of reaching and, more importantly, serving a broadly collective public, but it sought to experiment with entrepreneurial methods and systems of exchange to at least try to reach and serve that elusive public. My argument is not whether they sincerely (or even unconsciously) wanted to succeed, or if either peculiar notion of success would serve the public good. My argument is that Fluxus, as a way to interact with infrastructure, used and experimented with markets with larger goals for the community in mind. A portrait painter may have similar fantasies about reaching and impacting a larger public, but she does not expect to make that impact using distribution systems and markets as her canvas. Likewise, a small business owner may not see her efforts in relation to a larger market system the way someone involved with Fluxus might see playing with real estate markets as a way to change larger institutional patterns.

In terms of their techniques, different Fluxus entities sold shares (or tried to), and Maciunas and others intended the cooperatives as shareholding organizations, as were several of the Fluxus publishing enterprises (e.g., Willem de Ridder set up a "Society of staging exhibitions"). Ken Friedman, who taught at a business school, had also worked in a factory and studied the economy of the art market to better appreciate large-scale bureaucracies instead of a romanticized version of art and the artist. The spirit of Fluxus had always to do with taking art off its pedestal and putting it on a store's shelf. Their marketplace sought to make art and its meanings available to the machinations of the public. The more traditional notions of art as masterpiece allow only an elite aristocracy (whether populated by landed gentry or the super-rich) ownership and ultimate control over its meaning. For example, Yoko Ono and John Lennon designed a dispensing machine to dispense (with) art. A small selection of the many organizational struc-

dj readies

tures includes Dick Higgins's Something Else Press; Daniel Spoerri's Editions Mat; David Mayor's and Felipe Ehrenberg's Beau Geste Press; Daniel Spoerri's Eat Art Restaurant; George Maciunas's Mail Order Fluxshop, and AG Gallery.

Many artists associated with Fluxus constructed programmatic maps concerning cities, and they sought to use those mapping events to re-orient the map users' or event audience's, or, more accurately, participants' experience of neighborhoods and city communities. Wolf Vostell thought of the map as part of instructions to orient the city as a mixed-use site for music, visual compositions, and even the aesthetic pleasures of decay. For example, to advertise his *Cityrama* (1961), Vostell used a loosely painted map of Cologne, and for his *Petite-Ceinture* happening (July 1962) he turned a bus trip into an event by instructing participants to "keep a look out for the acoustic and at the same time optical impressions." He asked the participants to pay close attention for "décollages trovés," the "walls with placards torn or hanging down" (qtd. Wollen, *Paris/Manhattan*, 157). Aspects of a decaying city became the canvas for chance visual decomposition. From the failure of a city neighborhood, an opening for festival-like pleasures became possible.

For "Map Piece" (1962), Yoko Ono instructed the potential participant to

INTIMATE BUREAUCRACIES

> Draw an imaginary map. Put a goal mark on the map where you want to go. Go walking on an actual street according to your map. If there is no street where it should be according to the map, make one by putting the obstacles aside. When you reach the goal, ask the name of the city and give flowers to the first person you meet. The map must be followed exactly, or the event has to be dropped altogether. Ask your friends to draw maps. Give your friends maps. (Ono, 1962, printed postcard)

Like Maciunas and Vostell, Ono thinks of the city as a canvas and the social interactions and literal movements as the media. The map serves as programmatic instructions with opened constraints. Chieko Shiomi's *Spatial Poems* (1965-1966) included the following instructions under "no. 2: folding":

> Write a word (or words) on the enclosed card and place it somewhere. Let me know your word and place so that I can make a distribution chart of them on a world map, which will be sent to every participant.

Her instructions seek to set up social networks, and her chart will document the performance of her open constraints in something like six degrees of separation as the words appear all over a world map. Of course, the social networks reached by Shiomi were limited, but all of these mapworks suggest a Fluxus context for Maciunas's organizational plans for Fluxhouse Cooperatives, Inc. and Good Deal Realty Corp.

dj readies

On the one hand, many see Fluxus as failing in its mission to influence wider social networks and to enact socio-political change. On the other hand, I would argue that the social contributions they made not only influenced other artists working in, for example, conceptual art, video art, or artists' networks, but also contemporary conceptions of downtown culture. In that sense, the Fluxus brand is still thriving, and one of their canvases, downtown New York City, was, is, and will continue to be an international mixed-use neighborhood and marketplace. Reaching and changing the public explicitly depends on considering art production as an entrepreneurial small business (using mass-produced objects) rather than the output of a mystical artist-as-god using virtuosity to produce masterpieces. Fluxus hawked their goods, bought parts from suppliers, and packaged collective action and redemption in products for sale.

Many critics have criticized the artist-as-organizational-impresario as a peculiar failure of postmodernism. For example, Suzi Gablik argues that, "As organization and management penetrate further into the social order, there is no longer much difference between what artists define as their individual aims and what managers try to accomplish in their organizations" *(Has Modernism Failed?* 68). She sees this blurring of the boundaries between art and management in terms of the financial gains sought by individual artists. This "new psychological type of artist, the bureaucratic or organizational personality, lives in a condition of submission to a cultural and economic power system because of the rewards of money and prestige which are offered in return for such submission" (62). The problem with this move toward using bureaucratic norms is that it suggests a conformism and a lack of resistance among previously avant-garde artists and Modernist art groups.

Although Maciunas's rhetoric suggests the anonymous IBM structure in which all participants became anonymous contributors to the single corporate identity, Fluxus was in reality closer to the Bell Labs model in which participants were credited with particular innovations and works within the larger Fluxus project. Even Maciunas, who tried to produce his contributions to many works anonymously, now regularly receives careful credit for each and every aspect of his contributions. Many of the works were produced by a number of participants, and this aspect is still relatively rare in the art world. The individual contributions were combined into something much more interesting than any of the parts alone.

This way of working placed creativity and innovation in the hands of a linked or networked community rather than locating it in the mind of a sole genius in the form of a single artist's inspiration. Of course, this has political ramifications, and it may or may not have succeeded in negating or avoiding the art world's recuperative powers. This method of research resembles efforts to transform teaching away from

dj readies

individual achievement to group project-oriented lessons that increasingly involve larger networks of students.

Fluxus (as a pun on purging the bowels) sought to purge the art world of thinking of art as a luxury item with the elitism of museums and galleries, the money of collectors, the isolated transcendent artist, and the idea of great Art as the pillars that block cultural creativity. That purge was also a discovery using viral influence among participants as a new way of working. Things in the air were passed around and developed. The group previously known as Fluxus can now function as a generalized systems theory that experiments with the structure of influence and sociopoetic links.

In an issue of *Aspen* (edited by Dan Graham and designed by Maciunas in 1970-1971), Maciunas highlights this interest in new forms of systems theory. The subtitle of the issue is "art information and science information share the same world and language." A number of artists who were partially influenced by Fluxus participated in this project. Robert Morris's "Los Angeles Project" proposed a social art experiment that involves technology and information systems. The project situates cultural work as a new map of contemporary experience. Morris proposed to do an extensive ecological survey, of a selected area of Los Angeles, using multiple technologies from aerial photography to direct observation to infrared films. The survey would precisely chart the fauna and flora as they relate to changes in weather, humidity, wind, rainfall, geology, background radiation, and more. He then proposed to bury, and hide, high-output air conditioners and heaters and measure the effects on the surrounding area. The survey would continue in order to chart the impact of the artificial weather that Morris intended to create. In essence, Morris wanted to study artificially produced climate change about forty years before those efforts became central to ecological surveys. Presumably you could visit the site as a national park. Morris explains that what "miniature golf did for the game, this park will do for the national park system," as we would learn the impact of artificial climate change in a special park. The same issue also includes Richard Serra's "Lead Shot Runs" experiment, in which he dropped lead shot from an airplane and measured the size of the holes on the terrain below, and another work about landscapes from above is the documentation of Dennis Oppenheim's well-known ecological projects that includes photos of "cancelled crop" (a large corn field with a giant X shape cut in the corn field) and other similar crop art. These absurdist projects function as conceptual scores. They also highlight an interest in experimental procedures to change the way people understand the urban and post-urban contemporary landscape.

My reading of Fluxhouse suggests that one can adopt organizational and bureaucratic norms as part of a larger experiment in sociopoetics, and that this blurring of the line between art and life (or commerce) need not mean a grab for money and prestige nor a submission to a particular conformist personality type. Rather, Flux-house demonstrates how Fluxus might serve as a more complicated and nuanced model of what I call an intimate bureaucracy—that is, using the trappings and procedures of real estate management and official bureaucracies, for example, as part of a larger experiment in collective social and poetic forms of everyday life.

It is well-known that two of the key roots of Fluxus included the experimental pedagogy at Black Mountain College in North Carolina (during the summer sessions of 1948 and, especially, 1952) and

dj readies

The New School for Social Research (especially John Cage's seminars). Black Mountain College focused on a redefinition of the arts by stressing a holistic and experimental approach to art rather than a technical or formal approach. In earlier years, students had approached wider questions not typical of art schools; for example, they helped Theodore Reich build his first "orgone boxes," intended to focus sexual energies somehow leading to progressive social change. Although derided and later parodied in Woody Allen's "Sleeper," the boxes, which looked like futuristic outhouses, were an early attempt to combine the arts, technology, and a social program. The 1952 summer session added to, and changed, this experimental approach to art. Cage, fast becoming a major influence on the experimental arts scene, brought to the summer sessions his concerns with the I Ching and "chance" permutations in composing and performing music. His "Theater Piece #1," which assigned a specific time bracket within which each performer had to perform a specific action, became the prototype of Allan Kaprow's "Happenings" (see also Judith Rodenbeck's *Radical Prototypes: Allan Kaprow and the Invention of Happenings* examines happenings' radical potential).

Buckminster Fuller summarized the experimental nature of these influential summer sessions this way: "failure is a part of experimentation, you succeed when you stop failing." Although Black Mountain College eventually closed its doors, the teachers present during those two summer sessions (including Cage, Fuller, M. C. Richards, and Merce Cunningham) conspired to create a traveling school. They imagined, in Fuller's words, that their "finishing school was going to be a caravan, and we would travel from city to city, and it would be posted outside of the city that the finishing school was coming . . . we would finish anything . . . we would really break down the conventional way of approaching school" (qtd. Harris, 156).

Many other experimental schools have been associated with Fluxus over the years. For example, Dick Higgins and Al Hansen organized the New York Audiovisual Group as an outgrowth of Cage's classes at The New School, Jeff Berner and Ken Friedman were involved in the San Francisco State College Experimental College, and Friedman was later involved in the College of Mendocino. Of the nearly 200 experimental colleges and Free Universities started in the mid-1960s, however, few survive. These attempts at allowing for a laboratory-like atmosphere in the study of the arts and humanities were superseded by more mundane institutional concerns and those experimental colleges that developed in the context of larger universities transmitted their lessons and were essentially absorbed into the bodies of the larger institutions that supported them.

Even so, a number of educational institutions took a deliberately Fluxist tone. California Institute of the Arts—Cal Arts—began as a particularly prominent forum for Fluxus experiments. Fluxus artists played a major role in the founding faculty, and Fluxus people flourished there for a short time. An issue of *Aspen*, the "Cal Arts Box," documents some of this activity. The faculty included Allan Kaprow, Dick Higgins, Alison Knowles, Peter Van Rapper, Emmett Williams, and Nam June Paik. Although the laboratory atmosphere at Cal Arts quickly faded, participants like Paik went on to have an influence on many other curriculums and temporary educational situations, including Reed College, Evergreen College, Stan Vanderbeek's art program at University of Maryland-Baltimore County, Tuft's Experimental College, and mIEKAL aND & Lyx Ish's Museum of Temporary Art dj readies and Dreamtime Village.

Maciunas also planned the organization of a school as well. In a prospectus for the New Marlborough Center for the Arts, he described a think tank which would devote itself to: "1) study, research, experimentation, and development of various advanced ideas and forms in art, history of art, design and documentation; 2) teaching small groups of apprentices in subjects not found in colleges; 3) production and marketing of various products, objects and events developed at the center; and, 4) organization of events and performances by residents and visitors of the center" (Maciunas, "Prospectus").

One can apply intimate bureaucracies to social systems (such as IQ as a conjunction between collective and individual intelligences) and the paraphernalia used in those systems (such as intelligence tests) from an aesthetic or sociopoetic perspective. No one has studied IQ tests, beyond their intended uses, as intimate bureaucratic paraphernalia, as semiotic, or *semidiotic* systems, but others have examined psychological and psychoanalytic systems in terms of aesthetics.

Rather than examining how artworks reference social scientific experiments, we can examine how the foundational paraphernalia that determined, or tested, crucial aspects of identity (intelligence, wit, cleverness) owed as much to intimate bureaucracies, unwittingly or unconsciously, as to generalizable scientific validation or large-scale bureaucracies.

Intimate Bureaucracies

The WISC-R IQ test resembles boxed multiples, like Maciunas's "FluxKit" (1964). Both contain a series of puzzle- and game-like tasks packaged in small individual boxes inside a small valise. Both use tasks and instructions as a way to interact with the users. Once you open the corporately authored WISC-R valise you see a set of seven green boxes, square and rectangular, that fit neatly together. In among the boxes sits one small square book, and there is also a built-in folder in the valise top containing mazes and various other worksheets, plus a handbook for the test administrator. The series of tests includes five picture completion puzzles with increasingly more difficult challenges in figuring out how the pieces fit together to form a figurative picture.

The small book contains realist line-drawing pictures with something missing. The last box contains a series of cards organized under topics like "the fight." The partially unpacked valise resembles the FluxKit with its various boxes filled with puzzles, drawings, instructions, and geometric shapes. Looking over the puzzles and tests, one notices how the functions of art and design appear in the types, or forms, of the tests, and as a prominent thematic category. Illustrations in the test show images of an artist at work and the forms of the tasks throughout the test use art and aesthetics. As the historical context demonstrates, the importance of art is not new to this test. The illustrations of the test and the artwork above reinforce the observation that the WISC-R looks like an artwork, especially conceptual artworks like Fluxus boxes. There is not a direct line of influence between the test and the artworks; there were different artists and different goals. Nevertheless, the notion of intelligence quotients, and the design of intelligence tests, draws on art and aesthetic skills.

The function of the boxed multiples or series of

dj readies

tests plays against the notion of a singular quotient; instead, it suggests that an individual may have quick and clever responses to matching an illustration to a pattern in the colored blocks, but may have eccentric or incorrect responses to the narrative organization tests. As a psychological test, the result (a score or range of intelligence) elides these differences. In terms of the aesthetic form, the tasks and objects present multiple ways, outside of the appropriate responses, to illuminate "g." In the lingo of psychologists, the "g" indicates intelligence as a cognitive cause measurable with a quotient. One cannot help but think of it in terms of the g-spot or the "gee whiz" of the Eureka moment: rather than the correct answer, the pleasures of (artistic) invention (especially in appreciating concept art) emerge as prominent in the test's procedures. Processes from the test that directly relate to making art include:

- playing with narrative order;
- abstracting patterns;
- recognizing how the puzzles' shapes resist the realism of the line drawings;
- appreciating uncanny effects produced by leaving out details in realistic drawings; and,
- recognizing a connection between conceptual thinking and visual design.

The effects produced by the puzzles and tasks closely resemble Fluxus conceptual art because both art and test focus on provoking conceptual thinking. Both ask how an individual (in conjunction with a particular culture) interprets and organizes narratives, frames a situation, follows a labyrinth of choices, or fills in blanks. The two types of kits, conceptual art and intelligence tests, seem to share a convergent cultural evolution.

The poetics of the tasks in the WISC-R IQ test engages the user as it offers a series of constraints. Just as an artist leaves blanks for the viewer to figuratively enter the work, and just as one must attempt to fill in the blanks to find value in the artwork or visual poem, the WISC-R test provokes the user, visually and conceptually, to make a guess. For psychologists, the particular guess determines the viewer's intelligence. For the art historian, the particular effects and provocations determine the value of the aesthetic experience. As a test awaiting the taker, the WISC-R test remains open, potential, and aesthetically provocative for anyone not under the pressure to perform (or else), and who can simply appreciate the art and design. That appreciation does not simply catalogue the objects, but changes the stakes and the boundaries among the science of intelligence testing, determining a crucial component of identity, and conceptual art. Intimate bureaucracies need to borrow standardized systems of identity formation and testing as a crucial part of the social organization.

The FluxKit has a similar goal to the WISC-R test: an interest and fascination with challenging the user and playing to the intelligence rather than the emotions. After all, Fluxus was not selling soap or packaging products, in a salesman's kit, all in a valise, to show a potential customer the products. No, like an IQ test, the FluxKit was using Bauhausian modernism to ask for a much more intense, and intellectual, response to conceptual and aesthetic puzzles and problems. Conversely, the WISC-R contains art objects and sociopoetic situations all masquerading as intelligence tests.

dj readies

Craig Saper, *L.H.O.O.I.Q.* (2007)

The WISC-R test, sociopoetically re-arranged, as in my own example above, suggests an intimate bureaucracy that projects intimacy onto otherwise impersonal systems. This essay, and the illustration above of rearranging the tests, seeks to highlight the existing aesthetic relationships as well as the performance setting, distribution systems, measurement machinery, and social apparatus. It turns a crucial social program intended to place individuals into a standardized bureaucratic spectrum of intelligence into something like an inside joke or what Ray Johnson would call an "on-sending." It suggests an alternative to the low or high IQ in a pun on both low IQ and Duchamp's similar rearranging of the art world's spectrum of art from the sacred Mona Lisa to the vulgar pin-up.

In the 1960s, the artist Ray Johnson initiated a

practice he called "on-sendings" (see Bourdon; Johnston; Paik; and Pincus-Witten). He had already become famous, at least among a small coterie of art world insiders, for his collage works that included prints of James Dean and Elvis Presley. These works found him a small place in the history of early Pop Art, but his work soon moved off the canvas and into conceptual pieces involving mailing artworks to networks of other artists and art critics. His mail-art often included a repetitive line drawing of a bunny-headed character. These nearly identical hand-drawn bunny-headed "portraits" of famous people, each with a caption, suggested that one could substitute any head as long as you included famous or personally significant names. The characteristic look of these bunny heads also suggested that portraiture represented an artist's trademark as much, if not more than, the subjects painted.

Because all his portraits are nearly identical, his name-dropping stands out, as the reader inevitably associates the name under the picture with the cartoonish bunny-headed image. The readers care about the big "names" even as they laugh at the absurdity of that interest, considering the endless serial repetition. When you look at one series of these images and captions, or you are asked to function as the middle relay for a work involving Johnson and a celebrity, you laugh only if you recognize your own investment in this game. Otherwise, you simply discard the junk mail, fail to subscribe to the on-sendings, and focus your narcissistic fascinations on other stars. You cannot simply disentangle personal desire from mass culture; there is no utopian outside for Johnson. His work challenges particular forms of celebrity and identity formation.

In his on-sendings, Johnson would send an incomplete or unfinished artwork to another artist,

dj readies

critic, or even a stranger. Often these works consisted of Johnson's stamps and scribbles. A note, usually hand-written on the uncompleted artwork, would request that the recipient complete the work and send it to another participant in the network. These chain-letter artworks, which eventually evolved into more elaborate networks, depended on a relatively small circle of participants. Johnson would often involve famous artists, like his friend Andy Warhol, as well as influential literary and art critics, like Clive Philpott, in these on-sendings. Another variant of this process asked the participant to send the work back to Johnson after adding to the image. Much of his mail art and on-sendings consisted of trivial, small objects not quite profound enough for an art critic to consider them "found objects," and these on-sendings were previously excluded from art galleries.

The last twist in Johnson's effort to play through this perverse fan's logic (the logic that fuels the buyer's desires in art markets) involved calling or writing strangers. I think I received one of Johnson's calls after publishing an article tangentially related to his work. I do not know how he got my number, but one day my answering machine had a message on it: "Ray Johnson, Ray Johnson, Ray Johnson." I did not recognize the voice. Getting (or missing) a call from a relatively famous artist flattered me. Later, when I could not figure out who called me, the call began bothering me. Who actually called? How did they find me? Why did they call? What do they want? If it was actually Johnson, then what should I do with the tape-recording? Was this recording an artwork with lasting value? Should I salvage the tape? Had Johnson (or some surrogate) electronically mashed me (he often included images of potato mashers in his collages and mail-art)?

These works attack not just the art world's production of celebrities as a marketing device, but also the way this marketing depends on the fantasies, desires, and enthusiasms of other artists, including those in alternative art groups. To break the narcissistic link between the participant and the celebrity may in fact be impossible; Johnson's jokes depend on the link remaining strong. It works only if the recipients feel compelled to interact, participate, and link themselves in a (simulated) insider's network.

Johnson's fascination with celebrity also manifested itself in his formation of faux fan clubs, that also became part of his visual artworks, like the Shelley Duval Fan Club. Other clubs included the Marcel Duchamp Fan Club, the Jean Dubuffet Fan Club, and the Paloma Picasso Fan Club, as well as the Blue Eyes Club (and its Japanese division, Brue Eyes Club), and the Spam Radio Club. He even advertised meetings in newspapers, much to the surprise of the "genuine" fans. The kind of celebrity watching and stalking that Johnson examined pokes fun at art world celebrity-seeking, and these works put the reader in an uncomfortable position by highlighting the participant's fan-like fascinations, enthusiasms, and identifications.

On-sendings, in terms of a sociopoetic interpretation, use the procedure of mass mailings and impersonal chain letters in order to investigate and engender the intimate conspiratorial relationships found among artist, patron, fan, and collaborator.

dj readies

These intimate networks, especially in the art and culture-making world, use a similar strategy of using the infrastructural clues on their websites to engage the visitor in an insider's experience; that is, these art and culture networks make the driving force of the art world, insiders' conspiratorial pleasures and fascinations, available to a wider network of participants.

When the participant sends the on-sending, everyone involved participates in both authoring and reading. The distinction between artists and spectators blurs, not because of the open-endedness of interpretation, but because of the effort to build in interactive game-like structures of discovery and play. On a site for *Zine World*, the compilers describe why they created the site. The language they use to describe the process, and the inclusion of the reader's passions, enthusiasms, and love, suggests the ways the conspiratorial feeling is manifested in a description of the site's goals:

> We're passionate about the underground press. We give a damn, and we believe our readers do too. *Zine World* is written, edited, published, and mailed out by an all-volunteer staff who believe free speech is for everyone, not just for giant corporations. Nobody here gets paid; we do it because we love it. ("About Zine World")

Even in the information about ordering the print version of the magazine, they continue this same rhetorical frame: "*Zine World* is a labor of love, not a business." In their site's masthead description, the organizers of Invisible City Productions (game designers loosely affiliated with *Zine World*) also include the idea of the supposed secret machinations of the large and elusive collective of participants:

INTIMATE BUREAUCRACIES

"Invisible City Productions is a collective of game designers, writers, and artists who provide this as a space for the creators of secret media to come together and touch antennae" (see also the Wikipedia entry for "Prakalpana Movement").

Bad Subjects, a collective and magazine (see also the Wikipedia entry for "Bad Subjects"), has a website that lists both real and imaginary friends in the typical list of associated blogs and sites. The fan's logic, its simulation in an art game of the insider's feeling of connectedness, and its expression of these manipulations in both form (or interface/on-sending design) and content (in the description of the projects and collectives with terms like passion, love, and secret media), is a logic of a new intimate system.

dj readies

Some people think they might weave themselves in the rug and they put that line in so they can get out.
—anonymous Navajo weaver

... spoof their communications.
—Gen. McCaffery (ret.)

The parodic principle of deconstruction is to hoist the target on its own petard in a kind of mime of the host terminology.
—Greg Ulmer

The use of the oxymoronic phrase, intimate bureaucracy, corrects the residue of Romanticism found in the bolo'bolo manifesto. It does demand a paradoxical epistemology for use in the usually binary forms of social organization and politics (a mix of the trappings of faceless bureaucracies and systems of organizations with intimate artisanal DIY production). We cannot merely think about the paradox of the social organization that allows for the trappings of bureaucracy and the intimate pleasures of the inside joke. We must think paradoxically about the situation. The distinction is crucial. If we do not understand the difference between a positivism of paradoxes and paradoxical thinking, then we will fall prey to formalism and turn sociopoetic theory into an empirical method for only reading texts.

This manifesto investigates how to produce counter- or artificial communication. As soon as artificial, or infidel, borrowing starts, parody appears. After the mid-1960s, critical theory gained a new importance for a diverse audience of students and scholars. Among scholars in the humanities the conglomeration of linguistics, psychoanalysis, sociology, and philosophy became known simply as "theory." Something about the spectacle and drama of theory began attracting not just attention but love and repulsion. These theories examined how twentieth-century spectacles reinforced social control through a system of self-surveillance. Scholarship on spectacle emerged as an interdisciplinary field after the publication of Guy Debord's *Society of the Spectacle* in 1967.

Many scholars and critics, before Debord, had criticized mass media's hegemonic influence over the modern citizenry. Debord's achievement was to coin phrases for his provocative title and many other sound bites and slogans suitable for graffiti during the 1968 student rebellions in France. He produced a theory not only about how the world of mass media exerts social control, but also about how to intervene in the society of the spectacle using strategies similar to graffiti. He produced a manual on producing counter-spectacles opposed to the usually one-way state or corporate sanctioned spectacles. His phrases and slogans, (e.g., "In societies where modern conditions of production prevail, all of life presents itself as an immense accumulation of spectacles" and "Everything that was directly lived has moved away into a representation") soon became vulgarized in media reports just as he would implicitly predict in his work. In that sense he initiated the spectacularization of critical analysis. That strategic side of his Situationist politics remained dormant in critical theory until the last decade of the twentieth century. Before that shift occurred, media theorists

dj readies

shared only his suspicions and distrust of media spectacles.

Debord's severe critical apprehension of mass media's spectacles reached a pinnacle in the work of contemporary film and cultural theorists writing from the late 1960s to the late 1980s. In the 1990s, as the century came to a close, those interested in code systems began more explicitly employing the mechanisms of spectacle. They combined Pop artists' attitudes toward mass media and popular culture with the Situationists' pragmatic approach (detoured media communications that twisted the intended meaning of advertisements, TV programs, and news reports).

At least since the 1960s, the two scholarly approaches, critical apprehension versus spectacularization as a theoretical strategy, overlapped and intertwined. The theories that sought to unmask the spectacle created their own spectacular controversies and resulted in theorists-as-stars (Lacan, Althusser, Mulvey, Metz, to name just a few). By the close of the twentieth century, scholars began investigating how to use strategies borrowed from popular culture, like narrative, in their analyses of media codes. By the mid-1980s, theory began examining problems and solutions and also formed new disciplines, like "cultural studies." Theorists did not merely want to extend ideology-criticism's scope of explanation beyond cinema studies. They wanted to find a more stable and powerful institutional home in American universities. Film scholars often legitimated their discipline by reference to the theoretical foundation of their criticism. In doing so, they inadvertently made the value of cinema studies depend on the relevance of foundational theories (for example, Lacanian psychoanalysis). Once scholars re-evaluated and criticized how theorists *applied* psychoanalysis and poststructuralism, some scholars merely abandoned any effort to theorize film, while others sought to patch up the obvious problems. Film studies, threatened institutionally by its off-spring, cultural and television studies, and imperiled theoretically by wide-spread dissatisfaction with its methodologies, also had to contend with conservative attacks on its supposed lack of importance for college students.

For media and cultural theorists themselves, the productive enthusiasm surrounding ideology-criticism had faded by the early 1990s. Indeed, as the right-wing politicians began their dated attacks on leftist cultural studies, many media scholars had already moved on to other theoretical approaches. Media theorists began writing about the cracks in the edifice of ideology criticism. In spite of the corrections, vulgarized versions of media theory spread throughout the humanities, into museums and public schools, and thence into the angry minds of conservative critics. The theory had become conventionalized to the point of stultifying cinema studies. The situation was so predictable that an influential cultural critic half-jokingly fantasized that a *computer* in some publisher's office was covertly responsible for churning out these formulaic articles and books on contemporary media and culture. One could easily guess the outcome of a cine-semiotic analysis: "the representations of gender, race, or class are naturalized by an invisible style and conventional narratives." The problem was not that critical speculations increasingly lacked progressive political

dj readies

positions, but that their predictability muted their message. Theory had finally lived up to its worst critics' claims: it was boring—boring in the sense that it neither highlighted the otherwise unnoticed, nor allowed for new connections. It was a cliché.

Even in this apparently moribund state, media theories have to answer ever-increasing demands to explain a wider set of cultural-historical phenomena, including the events of September 11th. This situation created a pressing need for work that continued to highlight the pitfalls of previous theories and applications, and many Parisian theories imported into American media studies had as much authenticity and accuracy in this state of affairs as a Pepperidge Farm croissant. David Rodowick, Joan Copjec, Slavoj Žižek, Mary Ann Doane, and others would take film theory to task for its inaccurate (and misleading) use of Parisian theories (see References). In the 1970s and 1980s, film theorists sought to analyze the relation between cinema and ideology. Many film scholars initially greeted what was known as "apparatus theory" (the ideological analysis of the cinematic apparatus—both the literal and figurative positioning of audience members with the techniques, themes, styles, forms, and machines used to make and project movies) with productive enthusiasm. Times have changed. Studying contemporary film theory, as a way to understand media-cultural sociopoetics, may look to some like flogging a dead horse. There is increasing agreement about the inadequacies of contemporary media theory. Even Laura Mulvey, discussing the future of cinema studies, writes that the great challenge for film theorists is "to move to something new, from creative confrontation to creativity" (*Visual and Other Pleasures*, 162).

The best of the social scientific studies of

organizational structures do offer many important insights on electronic networks, but they (by definition) avoid the sociopoetic elements or aesthetics involved in networking as a practice (see Boetcher; Gibbs; Matei; and Wilson). How does an intimate bureaucracy create the impression of intense productivity and (almost) conspiratorial connections among an elastic group of participants (even including those just visiting)? How do these works manipulate participants to celebrate a type of group cohesion without the rules, restrictions, or enforced (or at least, fixed) identities required in cults, cells, cadres, and corporations?

The political practice of intimate bureaucracies, such as the OWS movement, both seduced and repulsed by centralized-planned cultural production as well as the exclusive coding of knowledge and practical skills as specialized and professional, seeks to build a collaborative exchange economy with a manipulative twist.

dj readies

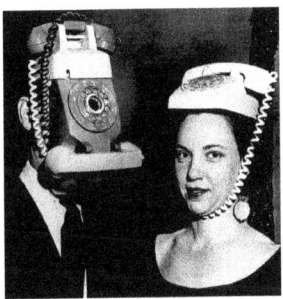

Call to (F)action

1. You form contingent, mobile, and other distributed weaves of networks as forms of autonomous intimate bureaucracies.

2. You answer and protest any evacuation of centralized governments' role and ability to defend, preserve, and protect. You spring to action whenever, wherever, and in whatever form state failure occurs, whether in its inability to respond to absolutely particular desires or in its inability to protect against its own brutal militarized police-actions and murderous demands to "tow the line."

3. You challenge incompetence masquerading as power, authority, and accountability by offering connectedness and shared autonomous responsibility to your networks' needs, desires, and happiness. You gotta live!

4. You celebrate underground alternatives to standardized solutions.

5. You use inside jokes and intimate poetics as a serious model for social organization.

Intimate Bureaucracies

6. You compose.

7. You embrace enthusiasms, links, movement, and the willing manipulation of desires (not for productive economic ends) to allow for tribe-making activities.

8. You notice the torque, *frisson*, and mood of those links and enthusiasms to prepare the mind for that type of imagination and intelligence.

REFERENCES

"About Zine World." *Zine World: A Reader's Guide to the Underground Press* [website], 1988: http://www.undergroundpress.org/about-zine-world/.

Aspen 1.8 (Fall/Winter 1968), ed. Dan Graham, designed by George Maciunas [loose pamphlets and pages, boxed; includes artwork by Robert Morris, Stan Vanderbeek, Carolee Schneeman, Dennis Oppenheim, Edward Ruscha, Richard Serra, Robert Smithson, and others]. New York: Roaring Fork Press, 1968.

Barthes, Roland. *Mythologies*, trans. Annette Lavers. New York: Farrar, Straus and Giroux, 1972.

Blom, Ina. "Boredom and Oblivion," in *The Fluxus Reader*, ed. Friedman, 63–90.

Boetcher, Sue, Heather Duggan, and Nancy White. "What is a virtual community and why would you ever need one?" Full Circle Associates [website], 2002: http://www.full circ.com/communitywhatwhy.htm.

Bourdon, David. "Portrait of the Artist as a Young Man," in "Returned to sender: Remembering Ray Johnson." *Artforum* 33 (April 1995): 70–76, 111, 113, 116, 122.

Copjec, Joan. "The Orthopsychic Subject: Film Theory and the Reception of Lacan." *October* 49 (Spring 1989): 1–28.

Debord, Guy. *The Society of the Spectacle*, trans. Donald Nicholson-Smith. New York: Zone Books, [1967] 1995.

Debatty, Régine. *we make money not art* [website]: http://www.we-make-money-not-art.com.

Doris, David. "Zen Vaudeville." In *The Fluxus Reader*, ed. Friedman, 91–135.

Foster, Stephen. "Historical Design and Social Purpose." In *The Fluxus Reader*, ed. Friedman, 166–176.

Friedman, Ken. "Fluxus and Company." In *The Fluxus Reader*, ed. Friedman, 237–54.

Friedman, Ken, ed. *The Fluxus Reader*. London: Academy Editions, 1998.

Friedman, Ken. "Introduction: A Transformative Vision of Fluxus." In *The Fluxus Reader*, ed. Friedman, viii–x.

Gablik, Suzi. *Has Modernism Failed?* New York: Thames & Hudson, 1984.

Gibbs, Jennifer L., Sandra J. Ball-Rokeach, Joo Jung, Yong-Chan Kim, and Jack Linchuan Qiu. "The Globalization of Everyday Life: Visions and Reality." In *Technological Visions: The Hopes and Fears that Shape New Technologies*, ed. Marita Sturken, Douglas Thomas, and Sandra J. Ball-Rokeach, 339–58. Philadelphia: Temple University Press, 2004.

Harris, Mary Emma. *The Arts at Black Mountain College*. Cambridge: MIT Press, 1987.

Higgins, Hannah. "Fluxus Fortuna." In *The Fluxus Reader*, ed. Friedman, 31–60.

Invisible City Productions [weblog]: http://www.invisible-city.com.

Johnston, Jill. "Between the Buttons." In "Returned to Sender: Remembering Ray Johnson," special section of *Artforum* 33.8 (April 1995): 70–76, 111, 113, 116, 122.

Kostelanetz, Richard. *Soho: The Rise and Fall of an Artists' Colony*. New York: Routledge, 2003.

Marcus, Greil. *Lipstick Traces: A Secret History of the Twentieth Century*. Cambridge: Harvard University Press, 1989.

Doane, Mary Ann. *Femme Fatales: Psychoanalysis and Cinema*. New York: Routledge, 1991.

Maciunas, George. "Manifesto on Art / Fluxus Art Amusement" [single page broadside]. 1965.

Maciunus, George. "Prospectus for New Marlborough Center for the Arts." In *Fluxus, etc. Addenda 1. The Gilbert and Lila Silverman Collection* [catalogue], ed. Melanie Hedlund et alia. New York: Ink &, 1983.

Matei, S and S.J. Ball-Rokeach. "Belonging across geographic and internet spaces: Ethnic area variations." In *The Internet in Everyday Life*, ed. Barry Wellman and Caroline Haythornthwaite, 404–30. Oxford: Blackwell Publishing, 2002.

McKenzie, Jon. *Perform or Else: From Discipline to Performance*. New York: Routledge, 2001.

Milman, Estera. "Fluxus: A Conceptual Country," in *Fluxus: A Conceptual Country*, ed. Estera Milman, special issue of *Visible Language* 26.1-2 (Winter-Spring 1992): 11–15.

Mulvey, Laura. *Visual and Other Pleasures*. Bloomington: University of Indiana Press, 1989.

p.m. [pseudonym]. *Bolo'bolo*. Foreign Agents Series, ed. Jim Fleming and Sylvere Lotringer. Cambridge, MA: Semiotext(e) / MIT Press, 1985.

p.m. [pseudonym]. "bolo'bolo" [transcription of a video], trans. Lisa Rosenblatt. *republicart.net*: http://www.republicart.net/disc/aeas/pm01_en.htm. 2004.

Piercy, Marge. "Utopian Feminist Visions" [transcription of a video]. *republicart.net*: http://republicart.net/disc/aeas/piercy01_en.htm. 2004.

Pincus-Witten, Robert. "Brother Ray." In "Returned to Sender: Remembering Ray Johnson," special section of *Artforum* 33.8 (April 1995): 70–76, 111, 113, 116, 122.

Rodenbeck, Judith. *Radical Prototypes: Allan Kaprow and the Invention of Happenings*. Boston: MIT Press, 2011.

Rodowick, David. *The Crisis of Political Modernism: Criticism and Ideology in Contemporary Film Theory*. Urbana: University of Illinois Press, 1988.

Saper, Craig J. "The Blog Report: Lack of Power in New Orleans." *Rhizomes: Cultural Studies in Emerging Knowledge* 11–12 (2005): http://www/rhizomes.net/files/issues.html.

Saper, Craig J. *Artificial Mythologies: A Guide to Cultural Invention*. Minneapolis: University of Minnesota Press, 1997.

Saper, Craig J. *Networked Art*. Minneapolis: University of Minnesota Press, 2001.

Shiomi, Mieko (Chieko). *Spatial Poem, No. 2*. Fluxus Word Events, 1966.

Simpson, Charles. *Soho: The Artist in the City*. Chicago: University of Chicago Press, 1981.

Vautier, Ben. "The Duchamp Heritage." In *The Dada Spectrum: the Dialectics of Revolt,* ed. Stephen C. Foster and Rudolf E. Kuenzli, 250–58. Iowa City: University of Iowa Press, 1979.

"What Is Bad Subjects?" *Bad Subjects: Political Education for Everyday Life* [website]: http://bad.eserver.org/faq/what_is_bad_subjects.html/. 1992-2012.

Wilson, M. "Does a Networked Society Foster Participatory Democracy, or, Commitment to Place-based Community Still a Necessity for Civic Engagement?" In *Citizenship and Participation in the Information Age*, ed. Manjunath Pendakur and Roma M. Harris, 372–87. Aurora: Garamond Press, 2002.

Wollen, Peter. "Mappings: Situationists and/or Conceptualists," *Rewriting Conceptual Art*. ed. Michael Newman and Jon Bird, 27–46. London: Reaktion Books, 1999.

Wollen, Peter. *Paris/Manhattan: Writings on Art*. London: Verso, 2004.

Žižek, Slavoj. "Looking Awry." *October* 50 (Fall 1989): 31–56.

Žižek, Slavoj. *Looking Awry: An Introduction to Jacques Lacan Through Popular Culture*. Cambridge: MIT Press, 1991.

INDEX

A
artisanal production 7
artist-as-organizational-impresario 32
artist colony 23
Artists Tenants Association (ATA) 21, 43

B
Black Mountain College 35-36, 54
bolo'bolo 12-14, 55
bribes 23-24, 26
buildings 17, 21-26, 28
bureaucracy 8, 11, 47
bureaucratic norms 33, 35
businesses 7-8, 23, 46

C
canvas 10-11, 25, 27, 29, 31-32, 43
change 23-25, 29, 35
Citizens for Artists Housing (CAH) 21
city 24, 27, 30-31, 36, 56
co-ops 25, 27
control 14, 23-24, 26
cooperatives 22-23, 26, 30
crowd 19-20

D
demonstrations 15, 19, 21
design 37, 39-40

E
everyday life 21, 35, 54-56
experiments 29, 34-35

F
failure 31-32, 36
Fluxhouse Cooperatives 22, 25, 32
Fluxus 15-17, 20-1, 24, 26-30, 32-37, 41, 54-55

G
governments 7, 12-13
groups 12-13, 15, 21, 34

I
instructions 17, 30-32, 39
invention, cultural 14-15, 56

M
mail-art 18-19, 43-44
manifesto 3, 7-8, 13, 28, 47
map 18, 30-31, 34
models 7, 9, 13, 15-16, 19
money 33, 35, 54

movement 15-16, 19, 21

N

neighborhoods 22-23, 25, 27-28, 30

networks 8, 13-14, 32, 43, 45

O

organizations 7, 10, 13, 21, 32-33, 37-38, 47

OWS (Occupy Wall Street) 10, 14, 19-20

P

participants 11, 15, 24, 30-31, 33-34, 37, 43-46, 51

politics 7-8, 10-12, 20, 47

power 14-15, 24, 27, 56

projects 8, 11, 15, 23-24, 34, 46

puzzles 16, 39-40

S

situation 16, 40, 47, 50

social action 10-11, 14-16, 21

social organization 12, 16, 19, 21, 41, 47

SoHo Artists Association (SAA) 27

systems 8, 10, 12-13, 19, 28-29, 38, 47-48

T

trappings 8, 10, 17, 35, 47

TriBeCa and Battery Park City 28

punctum books is an open-access and print-on-demand independent publisher dedicated to radically creative modes of intellectual inquiry and writing across a whimsical para-humanities assemblage. We specialize in neo-traditional and non-conventional work that productively twists or ignores academic norms, with an emphasis on books that fall lengthwise between the article and the monograph—id est, novellas, in one sense or another. This is a space for the imp-orphans of your thought and pen, an ale-serving church for little vagabonds.

<punctumbooks.com>

www.ingramcontent.com/pod-product-compliance
Lightning Source LLC
Chambersburg PA
CBHW070849160426
43192CB00012B/2375